621.43 Urquhart, David
URQ   Inglis
10279
         The internal
         combustion engine
         and how it works

DATE		
NOV 18 75		

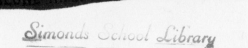

The Internal Combustion Engine
and How It Works

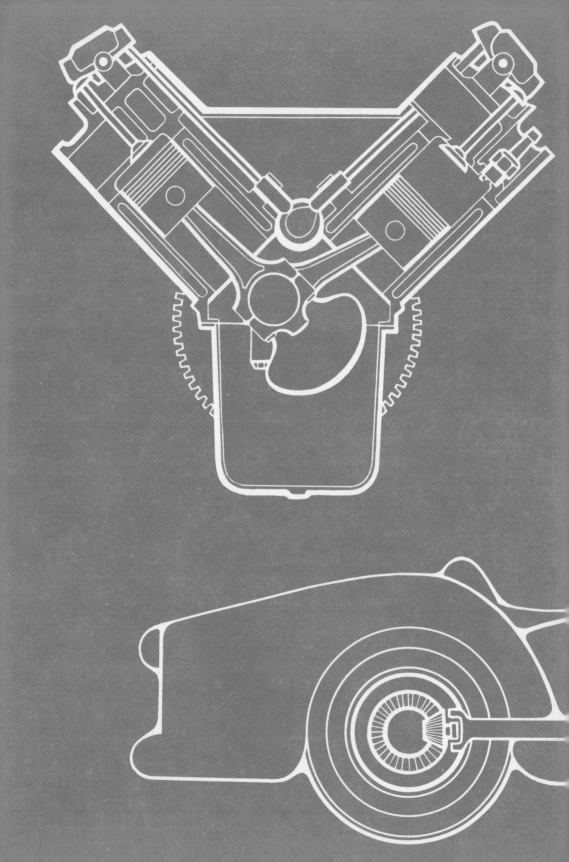

The Internal Combustion Engine and How It Works

DAVID INGLIS URQUHART

Illustrated by Eva Cellini

HENRY Z. WALCK, INC.   NEW YORK

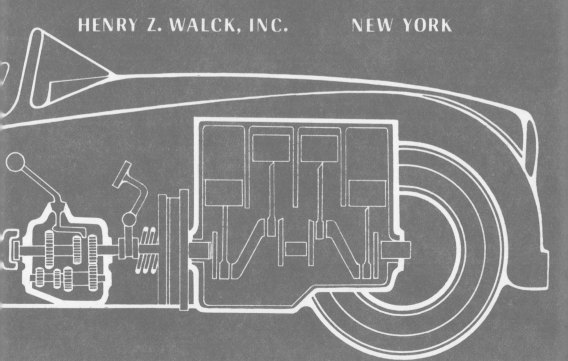

Text copyright © 1973 by David Inglis Urquhart
Illustrations copyright © 1973 by Eva Cellini
All rights reserved
ISBN: 0-8098-2095-1
Library of Congress Catalog Card Number: 73-7396
Printed in the United States of America

Library of Congress Cataloging in Publication Data
Urquhart, David Inglis.
The internal combustion engine and how it works.

SUMMARY: Traces the development of the in-
ternal-combustion engine, explains how it works,
and describes different types and their uses.
1. Gas and oil engines—Juvenile literature. [1. Internal-
combustion engines] I. Cellini, Eva, illus. II. Title.
TJ785.U7   621.43   73-7396   ISBN 0-8098-2095-1

To dear Priscilla, for twenty years of the best friendship and loyalty, and to Mac-Tavish—may he rest in peace.

Hugo

THE internal combustion engine is the basic engine used in many of the vehicles and tools that make work easier for us in some way every day. Almost every car, truck, bus, tractor, train and airplane uses an internal combustion engine. It powers motorboats, motorcycles and most lawn mowers and chain saws, as well as other garden tools. When you think about the services it performs, you might wonder how we ever got along without it! Yet this engine was developed for practical use less than a hundred years ago.

Before the invention of the internal combustion engine, man had to rely on other sources of power. He first used the muscles of his own body to lift and to carry things that had to be moved. But man's body, although a wonderful piece of machinery, is limited in the amount of work it can do. Man then used animals to help him carry loads, and pull carts and carriages, but still they were slow and had limited strength. Sailing ships and barges on rivers made his work easier too, but they could not help him do all the thousands of jobs he wanted and needed to do.

Man found ways of harnessing natural forces like running water and wind to do work for him. He discovered that water could be made to turn a water wheel which would pump or do other work. Wind could be used to turn the sails of a windmill, which would pump water or grind grain. Even today we use the power of the wind to move our sailboats and iceboats. In Europe there are hundreds of working windmills, but their uses are limited.

Even before the development of the internal combustion engine, man had discovered ways of putting steam to work. In ancient times he had understood that steam had power. When water is heated into steam, it expands or takes up more space. A mathematician called Heron of Alexandria invented an engine which used a jet of steam to turn a ball or a wheel. This may have been the first known use of a steam turbine engine. However, it was a Scotsman, James Watt, who developed the first practical steam engine in 1769. Although Watt did not invent the steam engine, he improved it so that it could be used efficiently. With the production of the

steam engine, steamboats, railroad trains and engines to run machinery in factories and mills became common throughout the world.

Steam was used to power an automobile called a Stanley Steamer. The Stanley Steamer was an exceptionally fine car, but it had one major problem that all steam engines share. It takes time to heat a boiler full of water to steam. The owner of a Stanley would have to start early; he had to build a fire under the boiler to heat the water and turn it into steam before the car would move. Today an owner of a car with an internal combustion engine simply turns a key in the ignition switch. This starts the engine and instantly the power to drive the car is ready to be used. Turning a key seems so easy but what is actually happening under the hood where the internal combustion engine is located?

Let's look at the words themselves: *internal* means inside; *combustion* means burning. An *engine* is a machine which performs work by changing heat energy into mechanical power.

In an internal combustion engine a fuel is burned inside a small space. When this happens, gases are produced by the burning fuel. These hot expanding gases take up more space than the unburned fuel, just as steam takes up more space than the water it is made from. The result is a tremendous increase of pressure or force as the gases expand. This force or power can be used to make an engine run.

To examine this principle simply, think how a bullet is fired from a gun. A small amount of gunpowder is burned or exploded inside the gun barrel. This creates expanding gases. These gases exert pressure on the inside of the gun barrel. They force the bullet, which is the only movable object, out of the gun barrel.

All internal combustion engines burn fuel. Your family car burns gasoline. In the early development of this engine, many kinds of fuel were tried. Actually any kind of fuel which burns fast can be used. Some experimental engines have even run on gunpowder, but they were not practical. As scientists and engineers developed larger and more powerful engines, gasoline proved to be the most efficient and practical fuel.

Gasoline is a highly refined, readily vaporized, fast-burning liquid made from crude petroleum. This crude oil, which is pumped or taken from the ground, goes through a manufacturing process called "cracking." It is a complicated process in which the heavy crude oil is heated and treated so that it will break down into many parts; gasoline is one of the liquid mixtures that results. Kerosene, lubricating oils, heavy tars and asphalts are some of the other by-products.

Gasoline is a good fuel, because it easily becomes a vapor. Then it has to be mixed with air to burn very rapidly or explosively in an internal combustion engine. This mixing takes place in a part of the engine called the carburetor.

The liquid gasoline is stored in a tank, and it is pumped or travels by gravity through a tube to the carburetor. As the engine sucks in fuel, the carburetor vaporizes the fuel and mixes it with air. Air is needed because it contains oxygen and nothing can burn without oxygen. The normal mixture in the carburetor is about fourteen parts of air to one part of fuel. When the fuel is mixed with air, it is then sucked into a cylinder. The cylinder acts as the combustion chamber or the place where the fuel can be ignited. The amount of fuel which enters the cylinder is controlled by the throttle or gas pedal. The throttle is connected to a flat disk in the throat of the carburetor which opens or closes to allow more or less fuel to enter the cylinder.

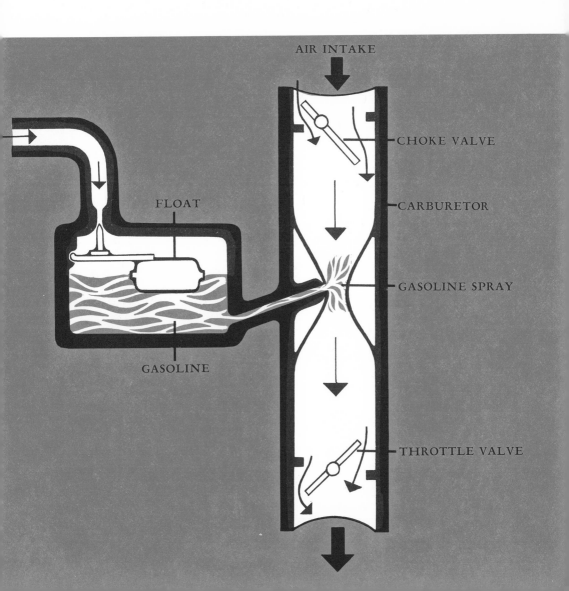

AIR INTAKE

CHOKE VALVE

FLOAT

CARBURETOR

GASOLINE SPRAY

GASOLINE

THROTTLE VALVE

The cylinder is located in a heavy piece of metal called the engine block. Most American-made cars have six or eight cylinders in one engine block. A motorcycle or lawn mower may have just one cylinder in its block. The block must be strong enough to withstand the heat and high pressure created by the burning expanding gases.

The fuel mixture enters the cylinder through a hole or port in the top or head of the cylinder. There is also a port in the head which allows the burned and expanded gases to escape. These ports are opened and closed by valves which look like metal mushrooms. The valves are controlled by a camshaft.

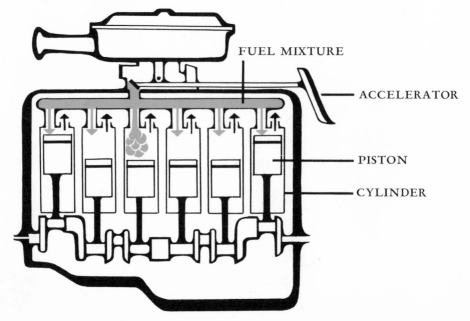

FUEL MIXTURE

ACCELERATOR

PISTON

CYLINDER

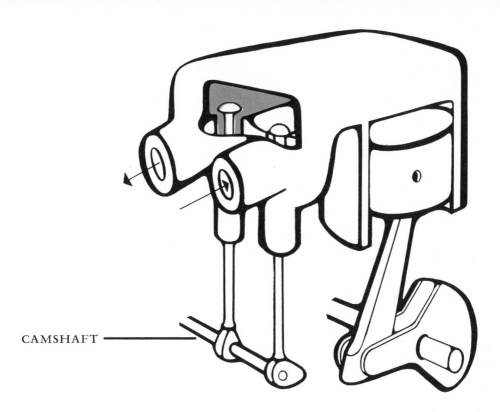

CAMSHAFT

A camshaft is a metal shaft which usually turns at half the speed of the engine. The name of the camshaft comes from the series of lumps or cams on its surface. These cams create high and low points on the shaft as it turns. Resting on these cams are rods which are connected through mechanical means to the valves. As the camshaft turns, it pushes the rods, and these operate the valves at the right moment to allow fuel to enter the cylinder or to let burned gases escape.

Inside the cylinder the pressure exerted by the gases moves a piston. A piston is a piece of metal which fits snugly but can slide in the cylinder. It is generally dome-shaped, solid on the top and hollow inside to allow a connecting rod to fit inside it. This connecting rod attaches the piston to the crankshaft.

The crankshaft is a specially designed metal shaft or rod, which is turned by the piston through the connecting rod. As the piston moves in and out of the cylinder, this back and forth motion is converted by the crankshaft into a circular one. In a car or any other engine-powered vehicle, the crankshaft turns the drive shaft which moves the wheels.

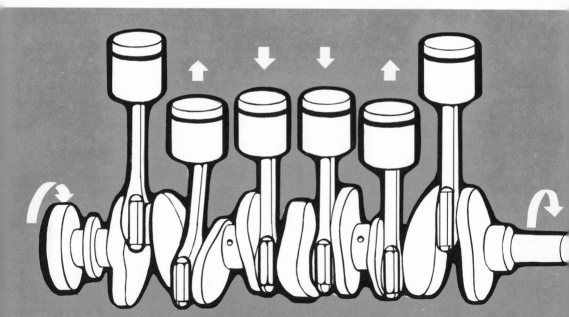

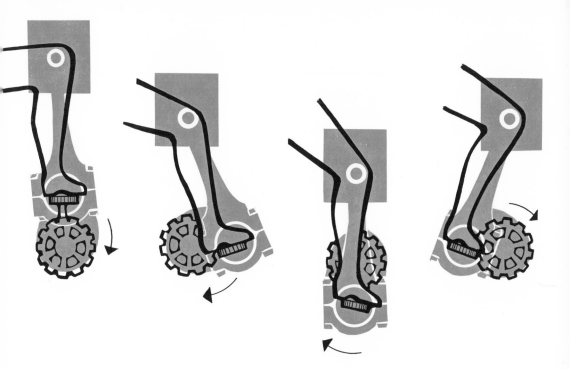

This same principle can be seen at work when you pedal a bicycle. The crankshaft is like the pedal. Your leg acts like a piston. As your leg moves up and down in a straight motion, the action of your ankle and the pedal changes that motion into a circular one. The pedal is attached to a crank which turns the sprocket and chain, driving the rear wheel.

All of these parts of the internal combustion engine have to do their special job at the right time to make the engine run efficiently and smoothly. This timing is particularly important.

The most common of all internal combustion engines is the four-stroke gasoline engine. *Four-stroke* refers to the fact that there are four separate strokes or movements of the piston inside the cylinder. The four strokes complete a cycle which supplies the power for the engine to run.

The first stroke in the cycle is called the intake stroke. As the piston moves away from the cylinder head, the space inside the cylinder is increased, creating a partial vacuum. The vacuum made by the piston vaporizes the fuel in the carburetor. The mixture of gasoline vapor and air is sucked into the cylinder through the intake valve which is open. Just as you inhale and suck air into your lungs by expanding your chest, the piston sucks air and gasoline vapor into the cylinder as it moves on its intake stroke.

At the end of this stroke the intake valve closes. The piston now moves back toward the cylinder head, reducing the space in the cylinder. As the space is reduced, the fuel mixture is compressed. Just before the piston gets to the end of this stroke, which is called the compression stroke, a spark plug ignites the fuel mixture. A spark plug is a metal and ceramic piece which is designed to make a spark inside the cylinder, and it is screwed through a specially threaded hole in the cylinder head. The spark plug contains two wire ends called electrodes, which are close to each other but not quite touching at the bottom of the plug. The electrical charge jumps from one wire end to the other, forming a spark. The electric spark ignites the compressed fuel and air mixture, causing it to explode or burn rapidly. This firing of

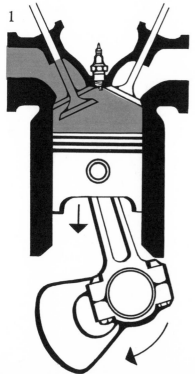

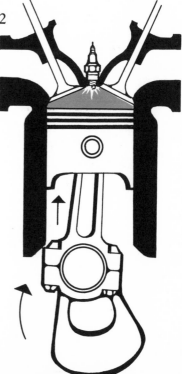

the engine creates a large amount of hot expanding gases in the cylinder, which exert pressure against the piston, driving it away from the cylinder head. This is called the power stroke.

At the end of this stroke the piston returns toward the cylinder head and pushes the burned gases out of the cylinder through the exhaust valve in the head which has now opened. The exhaust valve is connected by tubes to the muffler and the tail pipe. The muffler reduces the noise of the engine as the exhaust gases go through it. This fourth and last stroke is called the exhaust stroke.

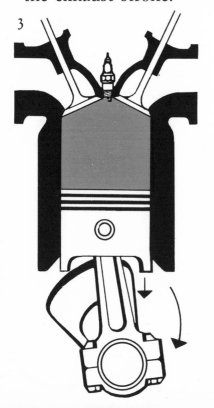
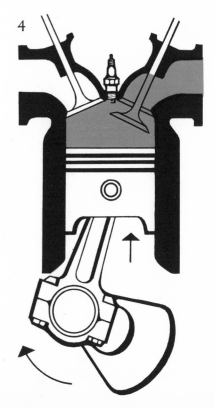

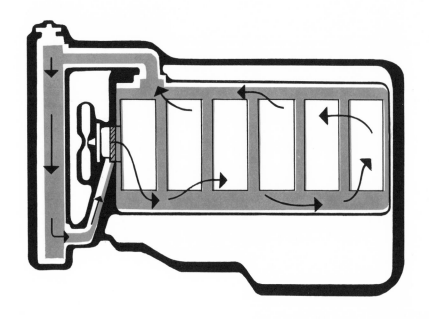

As each firing takes place, the walls of the
cylinder are constantly subjected to enormous
amounts of heat from the burning fuel. This
heat must be controlled by a cooling system. The
most common system is a water-cooled one. The
engine block has a series of passages which carry
water that absorbs the heat. The water is then
pumped through hoses to a radiator at the front
of the engine, where the hot water is cooled by
a fan and recirculated. This continuous flow of
water keeps the engine from becoming over-
heated.

Another kind of cooling system uses air. In an air-cooled engine the cylinder head and engine block are constructed with fins or projecting ribs which make it look like a steam or hot-water radiator in your house or school. The fins or ribs distribute the heat over a much greater area, and this keeps the engine cool. You can see these fins clearly on a motorcycle or lawn mower engine.

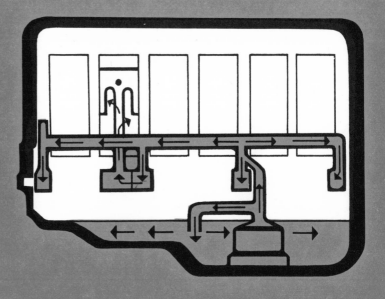

The parts which are constantly moving when an internal combustion engine is firing must be kept oiled or lubricated, or they would wear out very quickly. A crankcase or pan at the opposite end from the cylinder head does this job. In a four-stroke engine, like the usual automobile engine, the crankcase is filled with oil. This oil helps to lubricate the connecting rod and the points where the crankshaft is supported. While the engine is operating, oil is also sprayed up onto the cylinder walls to make the piston move freely in the cylinder.

Another important part needed in an internal combustion engine is a flywheel. As the power of the four-stroke engine only comes from the power stroke, or one out of every four strokes, that force or momentum must be carried over to the other three strokes. This storage of energy in the flywheel occurs during the power stroke. A flywheel is a heavy metal wheel which is generally attached to the crankshaft. When the engine fires, the power stroke forces the piston to turn the crankshaft. As the crankshaft turns, so does the flywheel.

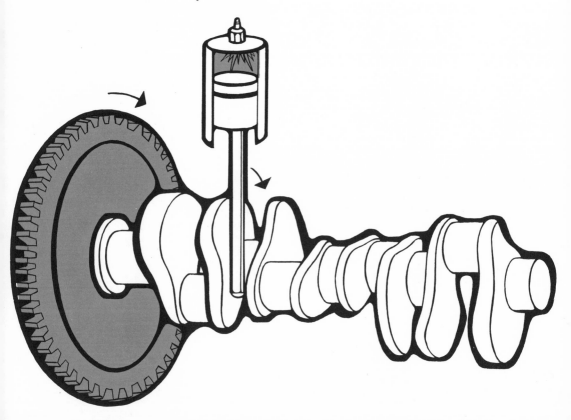

This principle of storage of energy is described by the word *inertia*. Inertia refers to the tendency of an object that is motionless to remain motionless and of an object that is moving to continue moving in the same direction. The flywheel when still tends to remain still, but when it is forced to turn by the power of the piston acting on it, it will tend to continue moving. This keeps the engine turning during the other three strokes, and helps it to maintain a nearly steady rate of speed. In an automobile the flywheel is at the rear end of the crankcase. Usually as the number of pistons in an engine increases, the importance of the flywheel becomes less, because the pistons can be fired one after the other and this keeps the momentum going.

For any internal combustion engine to work, it must have a means of igniting the fuel and air mixture in the cylinder at the right time. This is controlled by the ignition system. The heart of the ignition system is the distributor.

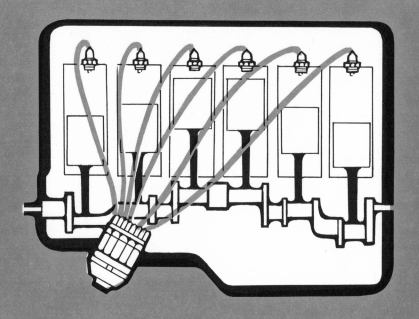

The distributor sends the electric current to the spark plug just at the moment that the piston is near the end of its compression stroke and when the fuel and air are highly compressed in the cylinder. In large engines where there are several pistons and cylinders, a distributor looks like a miniature octopus with wires, instead of tentacles, leading to the spark plug on each cylinder. Inside the distributor a rotor revolves which sends the electrical charge to the proper spark plug. Most engines use a battery as the primary source of electrical current and a generator which recharges the battery when the engine is running. Light engines, like hand tools and lawn mowers, use a form of generator alone as the weight of the battery would be too much.

The internal combustion engine in your family car runs on a cycle of four strokes, which are repeated over and over for each cylinder as they supply the power to operate the car. The four-stroke internal combustion engine is by far the most common engine used in automobiles, buses, trucks, motorcycles, tractors and even

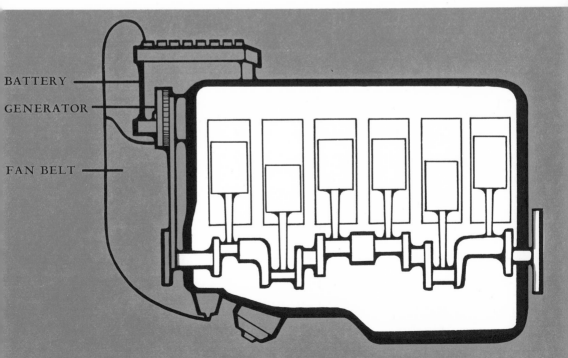

BATTERY

GENERATOR

FAN BELT

small airplanes. But there is also a two-stroke internal combustion engine which is often used in light tools like chain saws, small pumps, some lawn mowers and motorcycles where it is important for the engine to weigh as little as possible.

In a two-stroke engine the engine fires on every second stroke of the piston instead of every fourth. This provides more power for the size of the engine, as it fires more often, but it leaves a residue of burned gases in the cylinder. This residue makes the combustion less efficient. There are no valves in a two-stroke engine, but ports in the cylinder wall are opened and closed by the piston as it moves back and forth in the cylinder. The fuel is a mixture of gasoline and oil. The oil supplies the lubrication required by the piston as it moves in the cylinder. This fuel mixture burns less efficiently than gasoline alone and it leaves more of an unburned residue. A light two-stroke engine uses the crankcase, which has no oil in it, as a pump to force a fresh supply

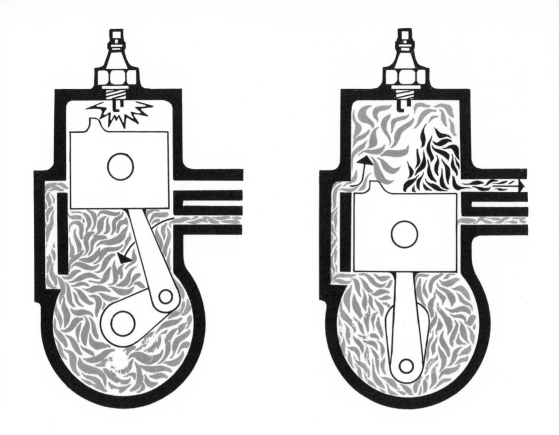

of fuel into the cylinder and then to expel the
exhaust or burned gases, just as you exhale,
forcing the used air out of your lungs. Another
disadvantage to the two-stroke engine is that
because it fires every second stroke it gets hotter
and has a shorter useful life.

Although in the United States alone there are
millions of internal combustion engines built
every year, it was not really very long ago that

the first practical engine was invented. The development of the internal combustion engine really started with the simple experiments of a Dutch physicist and mathematician, Christiaan Huygens, in the 1690's. He built an engine that actually burned gunpowder.

But it was in the 1800's that most of the work which gradually led to an efficient engine was done. In 1820 the Reverend W. Cecil, an Englishman, wrote about building an engine that ran on a mixture of hydrogen and air. This is believed to be the first internal combustion engine that actually worked.

In 1860 Etienne Lenoir, a French citizen born in Luxembourg, is given credit for building the first truly practical internal combustion engine. His engine had an electrical ignition system and a storage battery and was fueled by illuminating gas, the same kind of gas that is used for cooking in many American homes. This one-cylinder engine was built in some quantity and became widely used in France for industrial purposes.

George Brayton, a Boston engineer, built the first liquid-fuel engine in 1873. It was a two-stroke kerosene-burning engine, and it was exhibited at the Philadelphia Centennial Exposition in 1876. This was an important advance because the Lenoir engine had to be stationary since it was fueled by piped gas. An engine that was able to burn a liquid fuel could be adapted to a vehicle, as the fuel could be carried with it.

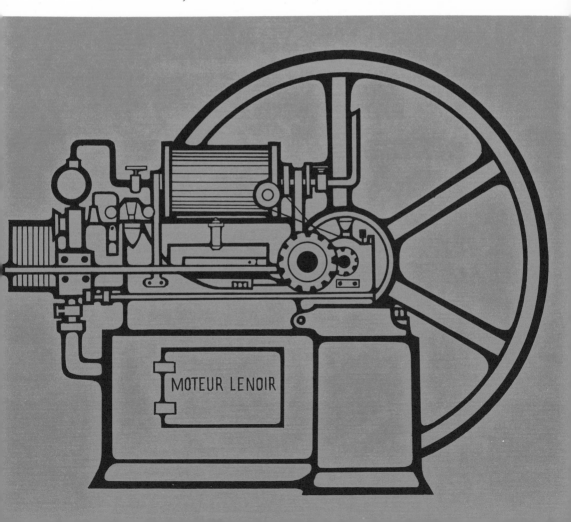

In 1864 Siegfried Marcus, an Austrian, built a Lenoir type of internal combustion engine which is thought to have been fueled with gasoline, and in 1878 Nikolaus Otto, a German engineer, built the first four-stroke-cycle engine which resembled the engines of today.

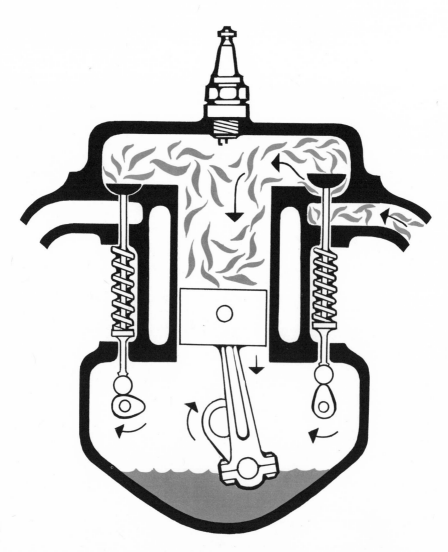

Finally, in 1889, Gottlieb Daimler, another German engineer and pioneer automobile manufacturer, built the first successful four-stroke engine that burned gasoline, had mushroom-shaped valves and two cylinders arranged in a V shape. This was the first practical and efficient engine, and from it most modern internal combustion engines have developed.

Several variations on the four-stroke internal combustion engine, that have certain advantages for specific uses, have been developed over the years. Large trucks, certain trains, and heavy machinery which requires a heavy engine with a great amount of power often use a diesel engine.

About 1892 a German named Rudolf Diesel invented an engine which could be used to replace the large steam engines that were in use at that time. This internal combustion engine was named a diesel, after its inventor, and it worked on a slight variation from the normal engine. The basic difference is that the diesel has no ignition system. There are both two- and four-stroke diesel engines. In each the method of igniting the fuel is to compress air until it gets very hot. If you pump up your bicycle tire with a hand pump, you can feel the pump get hot as you compress the air and force it into the tire. This is the principle of the diesel. On the intake stroke only air is sucked into the cylinder. The air is compressed by the compression stroke but it is compressed about twice as much as in a normal gasoline engine. This extra compression heats the air to a high temperature. At the point of greatest compression and heat, fuel is sprayed into the cylinder and the temperature of the heated compressed air ignites the fuel, thus producing expanding gases for the

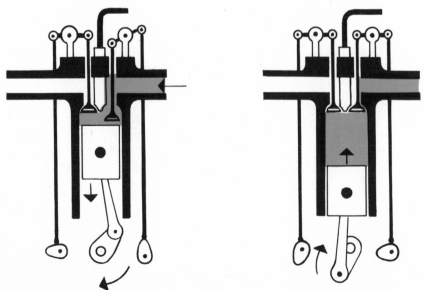

power stroke. The advantage of a diesel engine is that it is very powerful and can use a much cheaper fuel than highly refined gasoline. A diesel engine can run on cheap oil or almost any combustible liquid. The disadvantage is that the greater amounts of pressure and heat in the cylinders mean they must be much stronger and therefore heavier. Diesels are usually heavier engines and can be used where weight is not too important — for example, in stationary machinery such as pumps, or in heavy trucks, locomotives and bulldozers. Another unfortunate byproduct of the diesel is its fumes. As a diesel uses a low grade of fuel, it generally pollutes the air more than a gasoline engine, although both cause pollution problems.

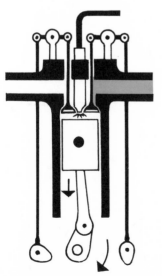 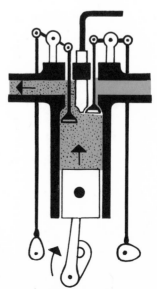

In recent years there have been some exciting new developments in internal combustion engines. One of the newest and most revolutionary is the Wankel engine. This engine was invented by a German, Dr. Felix Wankel, during the 1920's, and it may well be the engine of the future. The same basic principles of the four-stroke internal combustion engine are used, but instead of the piston motion being a straight back and forth action in the cylinder, the piston rotates. The cylinder is shaped like a very fat figure eight. Inside this cylinder a triangular piston, which is called a rotor, spins around. The tips of the triangular rotor are in contact with the sides of the cylinder at all times, and as the rotor turns inside the cylinder it creates its own combustion chambers. The size of each of the three combustion chambers changes as the rotor spins. The advantages of the Wankel engine are that it is smaller for the same amount of horsepower it produces than the conventional internal combustion engine. There are also fewer parts

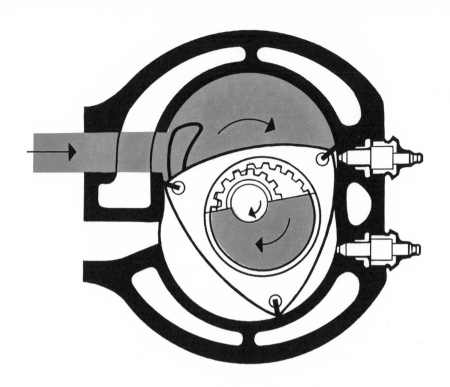

to wear out. There are no valves, no connecting rods, no camshaft or crankshaft. The connecting rods and crankshaft are eliminated because the rotary piston itself turns and because the power of each combustion need not be converted into a round or circular motion. The valves and camshaft are done away with because the ports for intake and exhaust are opened and closed by the action of the rotor as it moves by them. A Wankel engine is much smoother than the usual engine where the piston travels back and forth.

This action of the piston creates a much jerkier motion as the force of the piston is exerted first in one direction and then in the other. The rotor in the Wankel engine only operates in one direction as it spins around.

The Wankel does have some problems. The major one is air pollution. It is a dirty engine because it adds more contaminates to the air than does the normal engine used today. However, this pollution problem is being worked on now and there may come a day when most of the engines in automobiles, trucks and tools will be Wankel rotary engines.

Pollution is the major problem for all internal combustion engines. A highly industrial nation like the United States has millions and millions of automobiles on the road, as well as other vehicles such as trucks, buses and trains which emit fumes of some kind. So there is real concern over air pollution. All internal combustion engines burn a fuel, but this fuel is never completely used up in the combustion chamber.

Small particles of the unburned fuel, along with the exhaust gases which are in many cases poisonous, are expelled into the air which we breathe. Air pollution is a difficult situation which we must face. Not only is it dangerous to our health to breathe polluted air, but this dirty air kills plants and damages our homes. We are at last doing something about it. Now there are laws to control the amount of pollutants which an engine can send into the air. With all the advances in technology that our scientists have made, there is reason to hope that much cleaner engines will be developed which will do the work we want but not destroy the air we need to live.

There are two types of engines which at first may not be recognized as internal combustion engines. The first is the gas turbine or jet engine used in commercial airliners. The second is the rocket engine which has powered our astronauts to the moon and back.

Neither of these engines use pistons or crank-shafts or many of the other parts of the conventional piston engine. But they do use the internal combustion chamber and one of the basic principles of science called Newton's Third Law of Motion. The law or principle states that for every action in one direction, there is an equal action or force in the opposite direction.

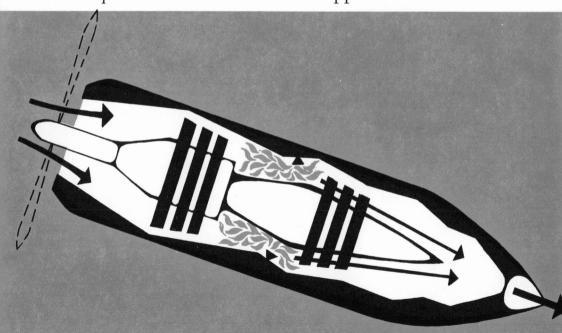

You can see this principle at work when you blow up a balloon and then let it go. The compressed air in the balloon will force its way out of the opening and the balloon will dart crazily around in the air. The compressed air in the balloon goes in one direction and the balloon goes in the opposite direction.

Both the gas turbine and the rocket use a fuel which is burned in a combustion chamber. The resulting gases are allowed to expand out of a nozzle or opening in the rear of the engine. The force of the burning gases blasting out the nozzle forces the engine or rocketship forward.

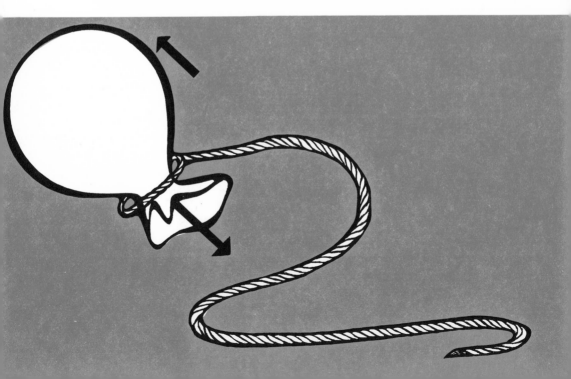

The difference between the gas turbine engine, which is commonly used in commercial airliners and military airplanes, and the rocketship engine is that the gas turbine uses air. It has blades or fans inside which compress the air. In the gas turbine engine the compressed air is sprayed with a fuel and is then ignited. As they expand, the gases turn another set of blades or turbines which supply the power for the compressor blades at the front of the engine.

A rocketship on the way to the moon has no air to use because there is no air in outer space. The rocket engine must carry its own oxygen and fuel mixture to burn. A simple rocket looks like a tube closed at the front end. The tube is filled with the fuel and oxygen in a liquid or solid form. The fuel is burned and the gases expand out of the nozzle and force the rocket through space.

For several reasons neither of these engines is practical for use in automobiles. The obvious reason is that the exhaust gases from both engines are extremely powerful and hot and would be completely impractical in congested areas like city streets. Another disadvantage to both the gas turbine and the rocket is that they are not efficient engines unless they are operated at very high speeds. Some attempts have been made to adapt a gas turbine to a racing car, but for the ordinary automobile they have not proved very practical.

It is hard to imagine a world without the internal combustion engine. There would be no cars as we know them, no motorcycles, gasoline lawn mowers, airplanes, trucks, buses, many trains and many other vehicles and tools. In the United States alone there are millions of internal combustion engines built every year for thousands of different jobs, which could not be done were it not for these engines. Perhaps some day another form of power with less pollution problems will be invented, an engine that runs on atomic energy, electricity or even the heat from the center of the earth. But until a better form of engine is found, man will have to rely on the internal combustion engine as the real workhorse of our civilization.

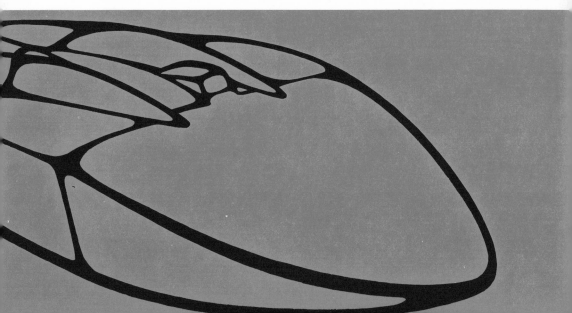